# The Disgusting Crafter

# make your own

# Fake Skin

## Julia Garstecki

**BLACK RABBIT BOOKS**

Hi Jinx is published by Black Rabbit Books
P.O. Box 3263, Mankato, Minnesota, 56002.
www.blackrabbitbooks.com
Copyright © 2019 Black Rabbit Books

Marysa Storm, editor; Michael Sellner, designer;
Omay Ayres, photo researcher

Names: Garstecki, Julia, author.
Title: Make your own fake skin / by Julia Garstecki.
Description: Mankato, Minnesota : Black Rabbit Books, [2019]
| Series: Hi jinx. The disgusting crafter | Includes bibliographical
references and index. | Audience: Ages 9-12. | Audience:
Grades 4 to 6.
Identifiers: LCCN 2017061648 (print) | LCCN 2018000058
(ebook) | ISBN 9781680726282 (e-book)
| ISBN 9781680726220 (library binding) | ISBN 9781680727586
(paperback)
Subjects: LCSH: Theatrical makeup–Juvenile literature.
| Skin–Juvenile literature. | Food craft–Juvenile literature.
| Practical jokes—Juvenile literature.
Classification: LCC PN2068 (ebook) | LCC PN2068 .G37 2019
(print) | DDC 792.02/7–dc23
LC record available at https://lccn.loc.gov/
2017061648

Printed in the United States. 5/18

## Image Credits

# contents

Did you know crafting in the kitchen is actually science? It's true. Making mixtures is something scientists do all the time. So grab your lab coat (or an apron). It's time to mix and measure your way to some fake skin.

# Chapter 1

## Be a Disgusting Crafter

Want to fool your friends by creating a nasty-looking **rash**? Or freak them out with a fake burn? Then you've come to the right place. This recipe will help you create the perfect fake skin.

# Chapter 2
# Let's make!

This recipe is super simple. You can use it to pull off **priceless** pranks.

# what you'll need

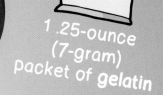
1 .25-ounce (7-gram) packet of **gelatin**

microwave

liquid skin-tone makeup

1 teaspoon (5 milliliters) water

2 teaspoons (10 ml) **glycerin**

fork

fake blood (see page 24)

small rubber spatula

microwave-safe bowl

## Directions

 Pour the gelatin into the bowl.

 Add the glycerin to the gelatin.

 Add the water to the bowl.

The skin is the body's largest organ.

**Microwave the mixture on high heat for 10 seconds.**

**Stir the mixture with the fork. Continue stirring until the mixture thickens. The mixture should be smooth and slimy.**

JOKE BREAK

Why are skeletons so relaxed?

Nothing gets under their skin.

Wait until the mixture is cool but not hard. This will take a few minutes.

7. Grab the rubber spatula. Use it to place the mixture wherever you'd like fake skin. Be sure to smooth out the edges. This step might tickle.

# CAUTION

Never use a knife to cut your fake skin.
You could accidentally cut
your real skin!

8. Let the fake skin dry. Drying will take about five minutes. It may take longer if you put on a thick layer.

**Dab** makeup on the fake skin. The makeup will help the fake skin match your own. You can then use tweezers and fake blood to create wounds!

## Using Your Fake Skin

When it comes to using fake skin, the options are endless! A good use for your fake skin is making fake wounds. The more **realistic**, the better. When pulling up the skin, be careful. You don't want too much skin sticking up. Once your masterpiece is complete, tell a friend you had an accident. Show your target the fake cut. Then enjoy his or her **reaction**.

**HINT**

Practice makes perfect. It might take a few tries to make your injury look right.

## Icky Itching

You don't need fake cuts to freak people out. Simply put a thin layer of fake skin on your arm. Be sure to let it dry. Then tell your family members you have a bad itch. A really, *really* bad itch. Start scratching at your fake skin. Pull your "skin" off before their very eyes. Be sure to make gross noises too!

# Chapter 3

# Get in on the Hi Jinx

Fake skin isn't just used for pranks and movies. Doctors create and use fake skin too. **Artificial** skin can be used to help skin loss. It can help burn **victims**. Who knows what kind of fake skin you might make in the future?

# Take It One Step More

1. How can you improve this recipe?

2. Tricks using fake skin can be a lot of fun. But sometimes they might not be **appropriate**. Can you think of any times you shouldn't play a prank?

3. Who else could artificial skin help? Do some research to find out.

# GLOSSARY

**appropriate** (uh-PROH-pree-it)—right or suited for some purpose or situation

**artificial** (AHR-tuh-FISH-uhl)—made, produced, or done to seem like something natural

**dab** (DAB)—to touch lightly

**gelatin** (JEL-uh-tn)—a gummy or sticky protein made by boiling animal tissues and used especially as food

**glycerin** (GLIS-er-in)—a thick, sweet, clear liquid used in making medicines, food, and soap

**organ** (OHR-guhn)—a bodily structure consisting of cells and tissues that performs a specific function

**priceless** (PRAHYS-lis)—delightfully amusing, odd, or absurd

**rash** (RASH)—a group of red spots on the skin

**reaction** (ree-AK-shun)—the way someone acts or feels in response to something that happens

**realistic** (ree-uh-LIS-tik)—something that seems very lifelike or real

**victim** (VIK-tim)—someone or something injured or killed

## BOOKS

**Farrell, Dan, and Donna Bamford.** *The Movie Making Book: Skills & Projects to Learn & Share.* Chicago: Chicago Review Press, 2017.

**Garstecki, Julia.** *Make Your Own Drinkable Blood.* The Disgusting Crafter. Mankato, MN: Black Rabbit Books, 2019.

**Winterbottom, Julie.** *Frightlopedia: An Encyclopedia of Everything Scary, Creepy, and Spine-Chilling, from Arachnids to Zombies.* New York: Workman Publishing, 2016.

## WEBSITES

Easy Home Recipes: Fake Burns & Bruises for Halloween
**radmegan.com/2012/10/easy-home-recipes-fake-burns-bruises-for-halloween.html**

Fun Sparks: Blood and Guts!
**www.science-sparks.com/2011/10/27/fun-sparks-blood-and-guts/**

The Skin
**www.ducksters.com/science/skin.php**

# TIPS AND TRICKS

Adults can be helpful. Don't be afraid to ask for help with any part of your disgusting craft.

To make fake blood, grab corn syrup and red and green liquid food coloring. Put 1 tablespoon (15 ml) corn syrup in a small bowl. Add six drops of red coloring and one green. Mix together to make your fake blood.

Need to make more fake skin? Simply double the recipe.